热带雨林

Sharing the Planet | Non-Fiction Series

Copyright © 2022 by Level Learning, INC. and Washington Yu Ying PCS™
Original and Edited Text Copyright © 2022 by Washington Yu Ying PCS™

All rights reserved. No part of this book in whole or part may be reproduced without written permission from the publisher.

Published by Level Learning, INC.
Content Contributors:
Washington Yu Ying PCS™ - Qianyi (Shirley) Zhang, Pearl Zao He You
Level Learning - Jingyao Qi

Illustrations by: Josh Taira

Leveling classification based on Level Learning standard.
For full description, visit www.levellearning.com

ISBN 978-1-64040-061-0
Simplified Chinese Edition

About Level Learning:
Level Learning provides a literacy focused curriculum specifically designed for K-12 Chinese as a Second Language classrooms. Our program offers 20 levels of specific and detailed objectives, leveled texts and passages, mastery-based online assessment, and analytics to enable data-driven instruction. Level Learning reading curriculum for both literature and informational text emphasize grammar and comprehension skills to help teachers develop confident and independent Chinese language readers. The non-fiction series of books are specifically designed to support our informational text course based on multiple national standards. To learn more about our entire offering, visit www.levellearning.com.

About Washington Yu Ying PCS™:
Washington Yu Ying PCS is a Mandarin English dual language immersion International Baccalaureate (IB) World school. Yu Ying's mission is to inspire and prepare young people to create a better world by challenging them to reach their full potential in a nurturing Chinese/English educational environment. Yu Ying's comprehensive IB, dual immersion curriculum equips students with global competencies for success in the real world. As a leader in immersion education, Yu Ying is determined to advance Chinese language programs and global citizenry education by helping other schools create and strengthen their Chinese programs. For more information, email: products@washingtonyuying.org

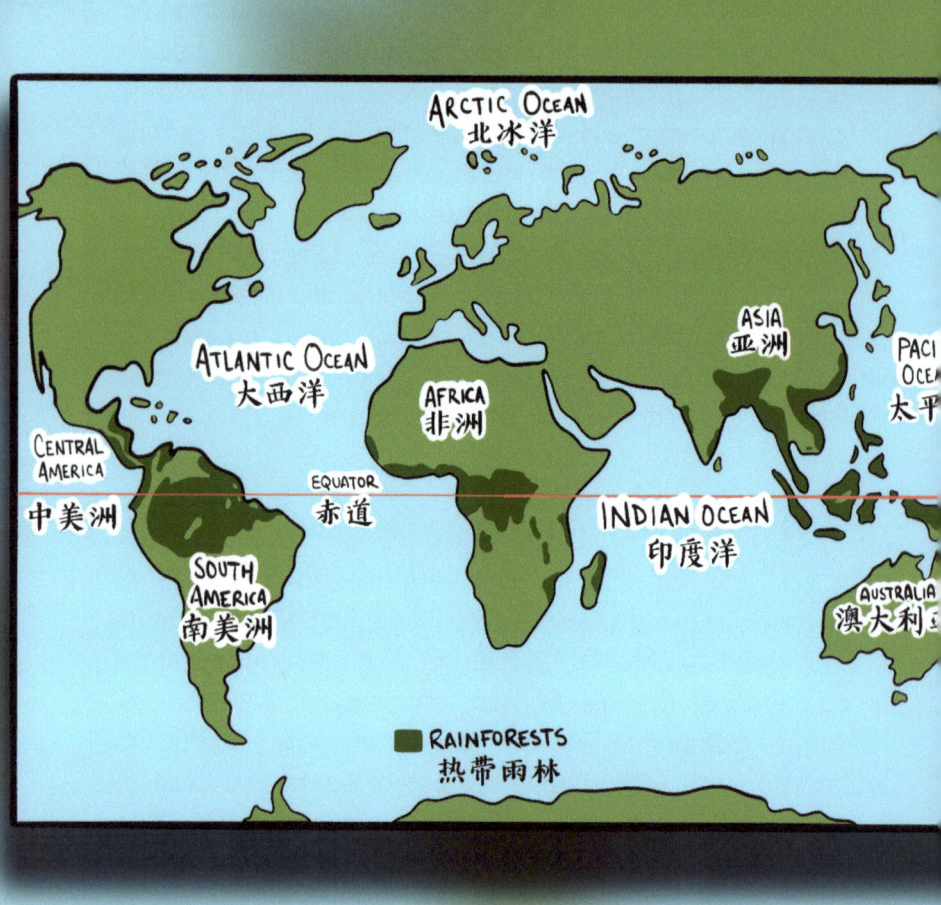

什么是热带雨林呢？热带雨林气候炎热，雨水充足，没有明显的季节变化。在非洲、亚洲、澳洲、中美洲和南美洲都有热带雨林。

虽然热带雨林只占全球面积的百分之二，但是在这里生长着全世界一半以上的植物和动物。在这里，你可以看到十几层楼高的大树，巨大的芭蕉树叶，以及各种各样罕见的植物。

世界上最大的热带雨林是南美洲的亚马逊雨林。它横跨9个国家，面积700万平方公里。这里是成千上万野生动植物的家。除了丰富的植物，亚马逊雨林里也生活着很多罕见的动物，比如说粉色的海豚，蓝色的有剧毒的树蛙等等。

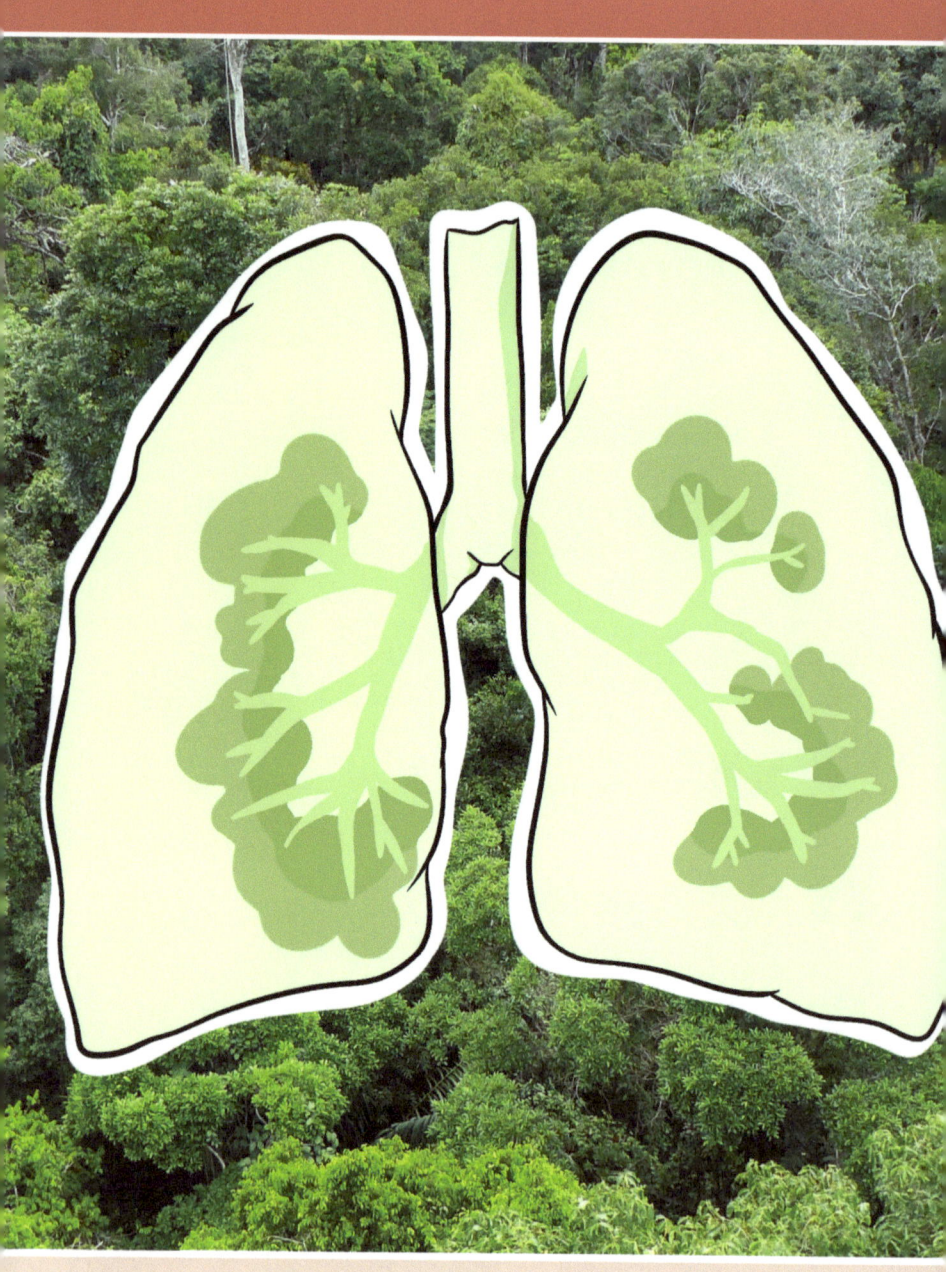

你知道亚马逊雨林被称为"地球之肺"吗?这是因为大面积的雨林吸收了地球上大量的二氧化碳,又释放出了很多氧气。就像人和动物呼吸一样,地球的呼吸要靠这些热带雨林。

然而，近几十年，热带雨林的面积正在快速减少。造成面积减少的主要原因是人们砍伐了大量雨林中的树木。其次，还有大面积的雨林被变成了养牛场或农田。科学家指出，如果亚马逊雨林消失，地球将会减少释放三分之一的氧气。

保护热带雨林，我们可以做些什么呢？我们可以节约用纸，比如可以多使用回收纸，这样就不需要砍伐那么多的树木来造纸；我们也应该减少食物浪费，特别是肉和奶制品，这样就不用把雨林变成养牛场了。

不仅如此，我们还要告诉身边的家人和朋友，让更多人知道保护雨林的重要性。让我们大家行动起来，一起保护珍贵的热带雨林！

Glossary

	Pinyin	English Definition
热带	rè dài	tropical
雨林	yǔ lín	rainforest
气候	qì hòu	climate, weather
炎热	yán rè	hot
充足	chōng zú	plenty
明显	míng xiǎn	obvious
季节	jì jiē	seasons
变化	biàn huà	change
非洲	fēi zhōu	Africa
亚洲	yà zhōu	Asia
澳洲	ào zhōu	Australia
中美洲	zhōng měi zhōu	Central America
南美洲	nán měi zhōu	South America
占	zhàn	to occupy
面积	miàn jī	area

	Pinyin	English Definition
百分之二	bǎi fèn zhī èr	2 percent
层	céng	floor, story
芭蕉	bā jiāo	banana
罕见	hǎn jiàn	rare
亚马逊	yà mǎ xùn	Amazon
横跨	héng kuà	stretch over
平方公里	píng fāng gōng lǐ	square kilometer
成千上万	chéng qiān shàng wàn	thousands and thousands
野生	yě shēng	wild
丰富	fēng fù	rich, plentiful
海豚	hǎi tún	dolphin
剧毒	jù dú	toxic
树蛙	shù wā	tree frog
肺	fèi	lung
吸收	xī shōu	to absorb

Glossary

	Pinyin	English Definition
二氧化碳	èr yǎng huà tàn	carbon dioxide
释放	shì fàng	to release
氧气	yǎng qì	oxygen
呼吸	hū xī	to breathe
然而	rán ér	however
快速	kuài sù	high speed
减少	jiǎn shǎo	to reduce
砍	kǎn	to chop
养牛场	yǎng niú chǎng	cattle farm
科学家	kē xué jiā	scientist
保护	bǎo hù	to protect
节约	jié yuē	to save
回收	huí shōu	recyclable
造	zào	to make
纸	zhǐ	paper

	Pinyin	English Definition
浪费	làng fèi	to waste
奶	nǎi	milk
制品	zhì pǐn	product
不仅如此	bù jǐn rú cǐ	not only
行动	xíng dòng	to take action

www.ingramcontent.com/pod-product-compliance
Lightning Source LLC
Chambersburg PA
CBHW041224070526
44584CB00001B/93